Psalms of Lane

Volume 1

Delana Pankey

Copyright © 2021 Delana Pankey

Poetry, Relationships, Self-Awareness, Grief, Frustration, Determination

All rights reserved. No part of this book may be reproduced in any manner whatsoever, or stored in any information storage system, without the prior written consent of the publisher or the author, except in the case of brief quotations with proper reference, embodied in articles or reviews.

All quotations remain the intellectual property of their respective originators. All use of quotations is done under the fair use copyright principal.

ISBN: 978-1-7948-0156-1

Printed by Lulu Publishing in the United States of America

Disclaimer: This publication is sold with the understanding that the author is not engaged in rendering psychological, medical, or other professional services. If expert assistance or counseling is needed, the services of a competent professional should be sought.

Dedication

This book is dedicated to anyone dealing with mixed emotions pertaining to grief, relationships and frustration. Throughout all the adversity that comes along with those issues, I have found determination within that helped me to endure. My hope is that someone is able to not only find themselves within this collection, but also gain the strength needed to reach their goals. I am a firm believer that transparency leads to transformation and I know that this collection has the ability to change lives.

Preface

From the desk of a broken-hearted girl who walked the journey of frustration and grief in relationships, but used her determination to find a way to fight back. It all started at age four when she lost her biological father who was murdered in a drive by shooting. Then, later she lost her bonus father at the age of twenty-eight from COVID-19. Not realizing how detrimental the role of a father was, she grew up with something missing. The identity, security and protection that is given from a father to a daughter was never obtained.

She struggled accepting and understanding who she really was, while feeling vulnerable to the world which caused her to create guards for herself. That was not the best decision, but it was what she used to survive. Experiences usually shapes one into the person they need to be while learning to embrace who they are truly meant to be. Although her trauma affected her tremendously, she knew that she was created to be something greater. There was a sense of urgency in her to become. Not really sure what that meant, she began to walk toward destiny receiving one confirmation after the other. The approval did not make her walk easier, only that much harder. Finding a way to stay motivated during the struggle was a new journey that she had to explore. The most prominent tools that was necessary was her paper and pen. She found that solidifying her thoughts was the start of her new beginning.

Table of Contents

Section 1: Grief……………………………...…9

Section 2: Relationships……………………....13

Section 3: Frustration………………………….26

Section 4: Determination……………………. 38

Lane 1- Grief

One month without you

Got me feeling blue

Wish we could just start over; anew

Wish time would just stand still

So I could have time to heal

And rebuild

What the broken pieces revealed

Living in your town

Without you around

Makes it hard to walk these grounds

Without a frown

As the days go by

I still contemplate why

We never got the proper goodbye

And now you fly high

I'm bending

But I refuse to break

There's only so much I can take

My only choice is to accept your fate

My strength is my weakness

My nights are sleepless

Masking the pain

Has become my new endgame

With disdain

I refrain

And remain

Through the rain

I pray for better days

While changing my ways

To make it through this maze

Not in a daze

Lane 2- Grief

Trying to reach

But there's no grasp

Trying not to dwell on the past

But happiness doesn't last

This pain

Isn't the same

It's so much farther

Out of range

I could never understand the deception of your health

But it was to save the reflection of yourself

In the eyes of the ones you love

Got the call at 2:38

It was late

All I could do was hesitate

And Contemplate

How God came to renovate you

Now that you're up above

Has made it tough

But the peace that you have gained

I know, will eventually fade the pain

Just know, your life was not in vain

Our loss

Was heaven's gain

And through your memories

I will sustain

God has prepared you

And I'm so glad that he shared you

Now that you are made new

I will attempt to be as prepared to

Lane 3- Relationships

To thine only be true

You laid your life down and said I do

For me, for you, til' death do us part

You gave a new start

Knowing the intent of the heart, my heart

But you didn't allow the wedge to keep us apart

You see

My life is not my own

But I couldn't right my wrongs

Until I was left alone

In the silence of my own thoughts

Your death was not in vain

I won't go insane

I choose to refrain

From worldly fame

To reach our heavenly gain

This decision wasn't given it was destiny

That is why I receive freely when you bless me

You never left me or

Second guessed me

Only pulled out the best in me

So, I let the rest be

I commit to you

The way you did to me

On the day they arrested you

From this day forward

I am anew in you

And the best part of me is you

That is why I choose to say those words

Back to you

I do

Lane 4- Relationships

True happiness

May not be in the cards for me

It isn't reality

To be swept off your feet

At a cross between

Where hope dies

And silent cries solidifies

The pain felt inside

To live a lie

Or in disappointment

For just one moment

Could true love be my portion

Dreams are not fairy tales

They may truly dwell

In the cage your heart resides

Even beyond your thoughts and minds

You can have what you see

Even become more than what be

Dismantling doubts

And finding faith will change the narrative

All hope isn't lost

I've counted the cost

And thought

I settled for what I bought

But realized

That those lies

Were fantasized

And that began to antagonize my mental

Being gentle and compassionate

Unmovable and one's steadfastness

Will help you obtain

Your love everlasting

Lane 5- Relationships

Old wounds reopened

Leaves the notion

That things haven't changed

The sounds of the ocean

Leaves my emotions

Calm, but also dismayed

This appointment

A failed moment

Created for two

Anticipating a new

As disappointment brews

How do we rearrange

And change

The pain caused by the same

As the cycle continues

Wishing this venue

Would become brand new

And change my thoughts towards you

Lane 6- Relationships

Blood is what connected us

You wouldn't know if you looked at us

Wondering where I messed up

Or how I even lost your trust

To be there is all I ever wanted

A shoulder to cry on

Someone I could get lost with

A shopping spree

No matter what the cost is

But that route took a tragic turn

One wrong move

A lesson learned

In this decision

I remain firm

I yearn to mend what was broken

Even thought about extending a token

But it wouldn't change the notion

Left by the potion

That were moving in slow motion

It takes two to tango

One can let go

While the other says no

And that enemy is still a foe

Open your heart

To the possibilities that be

Maybe a new start

Will set them free

If not, with me

Then, maybe their shall be

Lane 7- Relationships

Complicated

The first word that came to mind

But that is how it was designed

The proper connection

Did take time

Now, let's rewind

No, never mind

Why shed light on what's behind?

Never minimize what caused you pain

But try not to stay in the vein

Remember there's sunshine after the rain

So, there's no need to stay locked in those chains

Self-inflicted bondage

Does major damage

Obtaining more knowledge

Is the only way to absolve it

Forgiveness was the bridge that connected

That's why I opened my heart with no question

I'm invested

I'll just leave the past where it rested

The bond is now new

And so is my view

Support and consistency have been the glue

That changed the perception of what I knew

A renewing is what started the change

Along with actions that wasn't the same

Out went the blame

Started a new game

From this point forward

We have a new name

Lane 8- Relationships

I can't fight back anymore

Because your actions were poor

You aren't who you were before

Change what is evident

I'm aware

But who you're presenting

Isn't fair

Evolution coincides with maturation

The absence of both leaves you complacent

Which has me questioning my placement

Quick decisions have lasting effects

One thing I refuse to have is regret

I can't change my last

Only remove the mask of the past

As I make a step

Here comes another wept

I consistently lose progress

Because my mind isn't kept

I put my trust

In God I can't see

While continuously being let down

By the ones I can see

Don't do, Don't be, Don't say

But I don't see another way

Trying not to be afraid

Maybe this one I'll take to the grave

I'm brave

Not a slave

I choose to behave

And accept this vow

Until my resting day

Lane 9- Relationships

Thought I knew when to release

When to expose the beast

And how to keep the peace

But before I knew it my wrath was unleashed

How do you balance between suppression and expression?

When I share

You just stare

Why would I dare?

When your response declares your lack of care

Knowledge does not exclude actions

Although there may be passion

Your presence has been absent

At this point, I'm no longer acting

I'm just watching

Reading the captions

Fuel is needed for the fire

It's not about a want, but a require?

If you're not a liar

It's your desire

But, what is needed to inspire?

The test comes

To reveal what's hidden

To shed light on the trajectory

Of the decision

Are you satisfied with the life you've been living?

There's no reverse

Or a chance to rehearse

Take your mind off the worse

And break the curse

For the nurse

It time to give birth

Lane 10- Frustration

I'm slipping away

Alone

Need to call

But there's no phone

Truth disguised by tone

I know it's wrong

But can you handle my current zone?

Fear keeps me finding

New avenues to exist

So I won't miss

And fall into that level of bliss

The damage

Gets hard to manage

I'm famished

This is outlandish

Lord just tell me what your plan is

Purpose is key

To unlock what may be

The route to destiny

Sitting in a place called stuck

Where hard work just isn't enough

I know it's tough

But I can't give up

It's not about luck

But trust

Feels like if I sit any longer

I might rust or bust

But God says..

Don't explode

I'll lighten your load

Just stay on the road

That you were told

Waiting is different than being complacent

My destination could never be the basement

But adjacent

Because I was heaven sent

I am not longer bent

I've gone from went

And shifted to what's meant

Now, I'll just have patience

Lane 11- Frustration

From zero to one hundred

In an instant

Pause take a moment

And just listen

A sound mind will rationalize

Taking the time to recognize

Affords one to analyze

The truth behind the lies

To release or hold a grudge

Often times I do not budge

Because of what was

No matter what one does

But, who am I to judge?

Remove the gloves

Release, then love

Fly like a dove

Choose to trust the one above

Lane 12- Frustration

Take it back

Or wonder why

Was I the Lack?

Did I try?

Were questions asked as time flew by

Effort doesn't

Secure the outcome

The plan couldn't

Execute without one

Just like the moon without sun

Powder without the gun

The machine couldn't run

Functioned by the work of one

Who was I to become?

My future's yelling

Come get you some

While my thoughts say

I just sound dumb

Clearly, doubt has won

Regret and insecurity

Has arrested me

Trying not

To lose what's left of me

I have not many

But it feels like plenty

The weight hasn't lifted

I am not on empty

To rid me

Of these chains

Would eliminate the links

And change the game

Lane 13- Frustration

Seems to me

It's less about hard work

And more about happenstance

I've been wondering

When will I get my chance?

I know waiting patiently

Is what is best for me

This just can't be reality

It's not what I see in my dreams

Not trying to compare

But it's all around us

Moving past what's there

In order to plow the ground up

A short word

But the effort it takes

You have no clue

It's imperative to see the goal

While ignoring the distractions around you

For some it comes easy

For me it may not be

But one thing for sure

It's something we all need

Keep your eyes on the prize

Keep hope alive

Your moment is coming

All in due time

Lane 14- Frustration

I haven't been inspired

Maybe because I'm tired

Or I've lost the desire

I'm searching for my fire

What's placed within

Isn't just meant for me

It took a minute

But now I see

Why quitting just can't be

Motivation comes in many forms

From a smile given

Or a heart that's torn

It's the norm

You've been warned

Find a new space

And tap into the grace

That has been placed

Your only mistake

Would be letting it go to waste

Imagine if you never became

Only stayed in this lane

While stuck in the pain

How could you be used for heaven's gain?

I'll present my body

As a living vessel

No longer with me

Will you have to wrestle

My vision is clear

I have my gear

As long as you're near

I will listen for your ear

And give you the permission to steer

Lane 15- Frustration

I'm at my wits end

They say just begin

But now to pick up my chin

When I feel like quittin'

I understand the vision

And also the mission

I'm just looking for persistence

To reach it is finished

I'm tryna be silent

In order to understand the climate

I know emotions are fickle

Because right now they're yelling violence

Maturity is acknowledging the speck

Attempting to check

Preventing to regret

But also refusing to neglect

I don't wanna be around

But not underground

Maybe out of town

Somewhere lost with no sounds

It's easy to gain pounds

While chillin in a lounge

A mental vacation

That keeps one complacent

I attempt to give freedom a feel

But I can't allow chance to steal

I can accept the reveal

And heal

While protecting what I'm trying to build

Lane 16- Determination

Abandoned

Left alone

Restrained by fear

Kept me in the zone

Or maybe stone cold

To express

Created a stress

That tested my essence

And eventually overtook my presence

Captivated by hypotheticals

Revealed the medical

Justification, for my lack of explanation

Unable to obtain

Or gain

Due to the paint stain

Exuding through my veins

Winning the battle

Was imperative for the mantle

The first step

To lead by example

In order to experience

A piece of the sample

Lane 17- Determination

My voice is the pen

My words are the instrument

In place for the mission

To be fulfilled with good intentions

Eyes open

Ears wide

Waiting for a notion

Preparing for a sign

Our generation has seen a decline

Wondering why we've been misaligned

Making our way

Back to the grind

Will help us

Make up for lost time

We've missed the mark

Took our eyes off the prize

That's why our blessings

Can be a trap in disguise

Seek what's wise

Search and you'll find

See why a gift

Could be your demise

In fulfilling your purpose

Pick and choose what's worth it

The goal is to follow God's plan

Not be the one who hurt's it

Lane 18- Determination

The days and weeks are starting to mesh

Giving my best

Under this stress

Believing I'm blessed

While wondering if I'll past this test

This position is a part of the mission

My outlook may not be his vision

So, I'll just listen

And get in where I fit in

Understanding the assignment

Is needed before the call

Getting in alignment

Is necessary before a fall

This is your land

I trust your plan

Cause you are the man who can withstand

So, I'll drive with no map

Be a burrito with no wrap

Sitting on the lap

Of the one who does not cap

Be my guide on this ride

By my side you will provide

My life is yours

Continue to pour

I'll receive

What's in store

Behind every open door

With no hesitation

I trust your placement

Soon manifestation

Will be my destination

Lane 19- Determination

In the middle of a crossroad

A big decision

To leave my mark

Or be a slave to the vision

It was already predestined

From the beginning

I want to be right

In this life that I'm living

I need a clear plan

Given instruction

I refuse to be banned

Another deduction

Safe in your will

Is where I'll reside

Resting there

I won't have to hind

I know you'll provide

Because you have been tried

And crucified

Purposeful thoughts connect me to the divine

A reassurance I could not find

Now confirms I am aligned

When confused about the plan you were assigned

Seek and you'll find

A sign

That reminds

You of your purpose at this time

Made a right at clarity

And left confusion

Cancelling every negative delusion

Allows me to rewrite the conclusion

Lane 20- Determination

It's easier to self- destruct

To take a chance

Or blame it on luck

At this point enough is enough

Excuses are useless

A tool for the clueless

It presented as justification

But really just an explanation

For one's stagnation

It initially sounds valid

Because there's no malice

Despite intent, we still face this challenge

To wake up the sleeping giant

So comfortable in its cage

Content in its climate

Refusing to change its ways

To stop correlates with stubbornness

As halt with hesitation

Understand that reality is not a dream

Or a figment of one's imagination

The stage could be your lane

And not just a game

Designed like the same

To be another player with a different name

Divorce what you used to defend

Engage a new beginning

Marry the mission again

The goal is to secure the win

Lane 21- Determination

Time can seem like an endless line

Until you realize you can't hit rewind

Once you choose play

People fade

Along with the day

Then, we contemplate

Decisions that were made

Each given a limited measure

To maximize with pleasure

Or gain a treasure

What will you do with God's gracious gesture?

All afforded with twenty-four

A raised window

Or an open door

His ceiling should be our floor

He promised greater works than before

The permanence

Can be daunting

But an unfulfilled purpose

Is what will haunt me

I want to leave empty

Accomplish all that was meant for me

Bowing our gracefully

Knowing I fulfilled my destiny

A life with no regrets

Tracking my steps

As my best

That's how I know

I'm not finished yet

Lane 22- Determination

To only have one

It can't be taken for granted

It's because of the Son

We have this advantage

So, our time we must manage

At this day and time

People are falling like flies

Currently in my prime

Just happy to be alive

Being in line with the divine

Has my mind on rewind

When I sought a sign

Concerning my design

A goal with no plan

Is like a farmer with no land

Musicians with no band

All understanding the assignment

But, lack the execution required for proper alignment

Knowing purpose is a start

And pure intentions begin in the heart

But fulfilling the vision is the hard part

That's why gaining instructions prior to is smart

Along the journey of life

Continue to your destination

Keep pushing with all your might

And remember where to look

When you need restoration

Lane 23- Determination

Waiting on the world to be gentle

That's been eventful

Plagued my mental

In a world that's sinful

If I was good

I thought life would be

But I found out

That what's right

Isn't always what it seems

Distractions come to hinder your dreams

To dim your light

And remove your beam

Despite the fight

I remembered I'm a queen

Turmoil is just a reminder that I am royal

Without it the olive could never become oil

It's not a diaper that's soiled

But I'm marinating

Wrapped in tin foil

As trouble arises on every side

Choose to be wise

Don't go along with the tide

Instead vow to be a passenger

And allow God the freedom to drive

Lane 24- Determination

A car with no mission

Is like a goal with no mission

No way to execute the vision

Searching for momentum

While feeling depleted

A part of me yells

Abort mission, delete it

In a whisper I hear

The grind leads to gain

A rearrange is near

Just stay in your lane

Find the motivation you're seeking

In your heart that beats within

When your tank starts leaking

Remember why you started and begin again

How you start and finish is not all that matters

But, also the journey in between

Like how the glass shattered

Pick up those pieces

Everything you need is there

You'll find strength in your tribe

Through the one's who care

And if not through them

Seek ye who lives within

Lane 25- Determination

Why did their words hold more weight than mine?

A thought that weighed heavily on my mind

I had to rewind and find

What interrupted my original design

We weren't built this way

To be ran off of praise

To be fueled off of others

And the words that they say

Become your loudest cheerleader

In your audience of one

For the only opinion that matters

Is yours up under the sun

When the words stop

Your words can not

Their support is ran off of a clock

But your push is all you got

Be relinquished

From that euphoria

Because who knows

If they are really for ya'

Lane 26- Determination

The first time was accidental

Although I know it seemed intentional

Allow me to shed light on my mental

To see if my consequence could be gentle

I continue to stand on your promise

Even though if I am honest

This route I'm on is

Taking me the longest

I don't want my journey to end

Just prefer a new one to begin

Like the one I envisioned

Or merge the two to make a complete blend

A lesson I want to learn

Is patience until it's my turn

So that while I yearn

I still have my ability to discern

I contend with my thoughts

 Don't want to get lost

But did I really count up the cost?

I thought I heard clearly

Even confirmed the word was meant for me

But lately, I seem so far from destiny

This may be your test

Or just a stretch

Either or I'll present my best

Because here doesn't compare to next

Lane 27- Determination

To be the first

Can seem like a curse

No blueprint or example

It's up to you to leave the mantle

The weight gets heavy

My mind wonders if I am ready

But, I'll hold steady

And walk where you led me

I was chosen to be placed here

It's imperative I do it without fear

As long as you're near

I'll try not to shed a tear

It's often a path you walk alone

No one to answer the phone

They're silenced by your ringtone

To keep you focused and in the zone

Isolation doesn't mean exclusion

Remove that delusion

One is temporary

While the other is final

The first might be scary

While the second is simply denial

Embrace the cocoon

You'll be free soon

He wants to ensure that you're groomed

And, also finely tuned

Shift your perspective to gratitude

Change your attitude

Break the mold of the statue

While being glad that you were used

Lane 28- Determination

It wasn't clear

Maybe it was fear

That kept me from jumping that year

I didn't drive then

I let someone else steer

Took me a while

But, now my vision is clear

I'm the captain of my own ship

Not just a gun

But with an extended clip

Will I guard my whip

To escape from behind the gate

Before it's too late

I can't afford to hesitate

And revert back to that mental space

Fear can keep you beneath

Cause you to miss your peak

All because of your lack of belief

And the silence of your speech

Have caution

But, don't get lost in exhaustion

The world's a salad

But, you are more than just tossed in

We were brought in

Not knowing what the cost is

Lane 29- Determination

Fear has me frozen

Contemplating this potion

Wondering if I'm chosen

To go down this road again

It could be my destiny

Calling out to rescue me

Praying that God blesses me

In due time we all will see

The intake is so small

So, initially I build a wall

Even before I walk

I feel like I will fall

Still, I stand tall

And plan to conquer it all

I'm leaping

With no example to look to

I'll be the first

Embarking on this journey anew

In times where I'll wonder what to do

I'll remember, I rely solely on you

No one forced this move

I was given the right to choose

But, because you rule

And my trust is in you

There's no way I can lose

Lane 30- Determination

Value must be understood before it's presented

If not, you will fall into resentment

Feel like it's over before it's finished

Remember when Jesus told us, He meant it

Appreciation at home can be non-existent

But that can't cause you for forfeit the mission

My advice, stop and listen

To the one who first gave you the vision

Forget division and cause a collision

What seems like a disaster could be a new beginning

Words can push or pause

The stall will make you fall

And cause you to risk it all

Don't abort because of one phone call

Understand what's been placed

Then, their words won't stop your pace

It doesn't matter the obstacle faced

You will continue your race